Scottish Highland Adventures

Scottish Highland Adventures

Catherine Mackenzie

CF4·K

FOR LYDIA, ESTHER, PHILIP,
LOIS, JACK AND MARIANNE.
Repent and be baptised every one of you in the name
of Jesus Christ for the forgiveness of your sins. And you
will receive the gift of the Holy Spirit. The promise is for
you and your children and for all who are far off – for all
whom the Lord our God will call. Acts 2:38-39.

© Copyright 2007 Catherine Mackenzie
ISBN 978-1-84550-281-2
Published in 2007
by
Christian Focus Publications,
Geanies House, Fearn, Tain
Ross-shire, IV20 1TW,
Great Britain
Cover design by Daniel van Straaten
Cover illustration by Graham Kennedy
Other illustrations by Stuart Mingham
Printed in Wales by CPD

Contents

A Highland Welcome!

Welcome to the Highlands of Scotland where there is warm hospitality, magnificent scenery and wildlife everywhere – and that includes the people!

But even though there may be stories throughout history of wild Highlanders fighting their way through battles and skirmishes there is one thing that you can be sure of: a genuine Highland welcome is a warm welcome, even though the weather can be cold.

What do I mean? Well, the Highlands of Scotland are in the far north of the United Kingdom. They are well provided with high hills and large mountains. The temperatures on these mountains can drop drastically overnight, particularly in the winter. But the warm welcome is often referred to as a hundred thousand welcomes or 'Ceud Mile Failte' – the traditional Gaelic greeting.

Now don't get concerned. Highlanders don't have to stand there saying, 'Welcome,' a hundred thousand times. It's just a way of saying 'We are very glad that you have come to visit our land.' It's a descriptive turn of phrase that shows you how overjoyed people are in the Highlands to have visitors from all corners of the globe.

Descriptive turns of phrase like this are something that God often uses in his word, the Bible. One that comes to mind is when Jesus was with the disciples one day. Peter came up to him and asked, 'Lord, how often will my brother sin against me, and I forgive him? As many as seven times?' Jesus said to him, 'I do not say to you seven times, but seventy times seven.'

Now Jesus wasn't saying to Peter count out every time your brother is mean to you and then when you hit 490 that's it – he's finished. No. Instead Jesus was saying to always be ready to forgive

– don't stop. Seventy times seven was a phrase that Jesus used to show Peter that forgiveness is not something you give grudgingly – it's something you give willingly. Just as God willingly forgives the sins of all those who trust in him. When we forgive someone our forgiveness is small compared to the forgiveness of God.

When a Highlander welcomes you that is a small welcome compared to God's welcome to sinners who are seeking his forgiveness. In Luke 15:10 it says, 'I tell you, there is joy before the angels of God over one sinner who repents.'

If you love and trust in the Lord Jesus, one day Jesus himself will welcome you into heaven, 'Come ye blessed of my father,' he will say to you, 'My good and faithful servant.'

Mountain Mayhem

The Highlands of Scotland are home to the highest mountain in the United Kingdom: Ben Nevis. It begins its rise from sea-level on the shores of Loch Linnhe, to tower at 1,344 metres. So although it isn't as high as other mountains in other countries it is a mountain that attracts many hikers from around the world. I even heard that someone climbed it pushing a piano in order to raise money for charity.

Now although Ben Nevis isn't as high as Alpine mountains, it is on a more northerly latitude and the climate can get very cold, very quickly. If you were to begin your day on the shores of Loch Linnhe it might be quite mild but by the time you reach the summit of the Ben the wind could be bitter and chilling. So, if you are walking up the mountain footpath be prepared for bad weather – even if the sun is shining! The weather on top of the mountains is not always tolerant of the inexperienced and unprepared hiker.

Jesus told a story about some bridesmaids. Some of them were ready for the wedding ceremony. Some were not. The bridesmaids had just gone off to bed to await the arrival of the bridegroom as was the custom in Bible times. It was pitch-black outside. There were no street lights to brighten the dark corners and alleyways. So when the groom arrived the girls had to jump out of bed and get themselves ready to go into the dark. However, five of the bridesmaids had forgotten to fill their lamps with oil. Desperate, they pleaded with the others to give them some oil, but the other girls only had enough oil for their own lamps. The forgetful girls ran to the market to buy more oil while the wedding party went on its way. When the forgetful girls finally arrived at the groom's house the door was locked. They were too late to get into the festivities.

Jesus used this story to illustrate a simple but important fact. We must all be ready for the day when we will meet God. The foolish bridesmaids were not ready to meet the bridegroom. The foolish hiker is not ready to meet with bad weather. Some people will not be ready to meet Jesus. When they die they will not have trusted in Jesus to save them from their sins. They will die unprepared. They will be lost.

Why is sin punished like this? It is because God is perfect, there is nothing evil about him. Everything he does is fair and just. He made a beautiful perfect world for humans to live in. But from

the beginning humanity has spoiled that world by disobeying God's instructions. Sin must be punished but because God loved the world so much Jesus Christ had to take the punishment instead. When Jesus was on the Cross God put all his anger and hatred for sin onto his own dear son.

Think about that. Look at what Jesus had to go through to cure sin. He had to suffer like no one has ever suffered or ever will. That shows us how terrible sin is.

If you are planning a holiday or a trip away somewhere with your family or school you will need to make a list of what to take with you. It can be complicated to work out all that you need. If you are planning a mountain hike it is dangerous if you forget to take a compass! If you forget your compass you might find that you are headed in the wrong direction and then you'll get completely lost.

It is dangerous if you are not ready to meet Jesus. If you die without forgiveness of sins then you are truly lost. All sin deserves God's anger. Sin has poisoned the world and our hearts so that we want to sin instead of pleasing God. It is only Jesus Christ who can cure us from the poison of sin and make us willing to please God instead.

So this brings us back to Ben Nevis. Do you know what the word Nevis means? In Gaelic the mountain's name, Beinn Nibheis, means poisonous or terrible. If you are out on that mountain when the sun is shining then it might seem strange to call the mountain poisonous. But in the middle of a storm, when the sky is dark and you have lost your way – you would definitely call the mountain a whole host of horrible names!

Sometimes sin doesn't seem to be the dreadful thing that it really is. Sin deceives us into thinking that disobeying God is fun and enjoyable. When you are doing what you please and disobeying God you might not think that the sins you are doing are dangerous.

Ignoring God's word means that you are in more danger than someone who is missing in the thick of a blizzard.

A Beautiful Language

Everyone loves to speak their own language. Perhaps you've never thought about it before – but if you had to leave your homeland and go to live in another country, not knowing when or if you would ever return you would long to be able to speak to other people in the language that you know best.

If you live in the Highlands of Scotland or if you are visiting as a tourist you will notice that there are road signs with names like Achiltibuie, Brora, Culloden, Dunkeld ... there are unusual sounding places to discover as you travel around. Most road signs have two names for each place. That is because there are two official languages in Scotland – English and Gaelic. Gaelic was the language in the Highlands of Scotland for hundreds of years. There are still Gaelic speaking schools in some towns and cities and there are even now Gaelic radio and television programmes. Nowadays, however, most people in Scotland speak English – although they speak it with a Scottish accent.

If you were welcoming someone to the Highlands of Scotland and you spoke Gaelic you would say, 'Failte gu Gaidhealtachd na h-Alba'. Alba is the old Celtic name for Scotland. Look out for Gaelic words when you are visiting or walking around the Highlands. See if you can find out the Gaelic names of the places that you visit.

If you don't have plans to visit us just yet, don't worry – perhaps you can find out the meaning of the place that you live in. Most place names have meanings. The capital of the Highlands is called Inverness – and this means mouth of the Ness, because the city is situated at the mouth of the River Ness.

The Gaelic language is one that isn't spoken as much as it used to be two hundred years ago. But it is still spoken in different places. Today you will hear Gaelic spoken mostly in the far north west of Scotland, particularly in the Islands of Lewis, Harris and Skye, but it is also spoken in other parts of the world where Gaelic speaking people emigrated to. For example in America and Canada you will find groups of people who still speak Gaelic as their first language. You will even find Gaelic speakers in South America in countries like Chile. Scottish people have travelled the globe in search of work, land and religious freedom.

Sometimes people speak about the language of love. When they talk about that they aren't really talking about someone saying the words 'I love you.' They are really talking about actions rather than words. When someone is talking the language of love it means that they are doing things that are loving and lovely. Perhaps you think love is a sissy word – just for Valentines day. That is so wrong. Love is much more than hearts and flowers. Love is a strong word – love is a word that can change the world if it is done properly.

Jesus Christ is the best example of someone who spoke the

language of love – and he spoke it with strength. He didn't just speak it with words, his actions showed love – more love than anyone before or since.

In the Bible we read in John 15:13 that there is no greater love than when someone lays down his life for his friends. This is exactly what Jesus did – but he lay down his life for sinners, for people who hated him, not for people who loved him like friends. Jesus' love is so great that even when his people were sinners, hating God instead of wanting to please him, Jesus loved them still.

The Gaelic language is one of a set of Celtic languages that exist in a few different countries. For example the Welsh language is a Celtic language, as is Breton in France and the Gaelic spoken in Ireland. The languages are similar in some ways and very different in others. Often if you learn a language when you are older you never sound the same as someone who has learned the language from their earliest days. Someone who is a fluent native speaker in a language can listen to you speaking that language and tell quite easily that you normally speak a different language.

There is a story in the Bible about a fight between two groups of people, the Gileadites and the Ephraimites. The story running up to the battle is a bit complicated. The Ephraimites, however, were in the wrong and the two groups went to war over it. The Ephraimites began insulting the Gileadites and there was a battle. The Gilead troops captured some strategic fords at Jordan and when the Ephraim fugitives wanted to cross over they had to pretend that they weren't Ephraimites at all. But the Ephraimites could not pronounce the word 'Shibboleth' properly, however hard they tried. So the Gilead soldiers asked everyone crossing the Jordan to say the word 'Shibboleth' – if they couldn't say it then they were captured and killed.

Can people tell what country you are from when they hear you speak, or what part of the country you are from? Do you think people can tell if you are a Christian or not by the words you say?

If you follow Christ you will speak words that show how lovely Christ is – you will encourage others to follow Christ too.

Scotland and the Highlands of Scotland used to be known in other countries as The Land of the Book – this meant that Scotland was The Land of the Bible. People might have been able to tell you were from Scotland by your accent – but in the past people would have also known that many Scottish people believed the word of God. Scottish people used to read God's word a lot. They cared about what God said. They wanted to obey him. But over the years many people stopped doing this. They stopped reading and listening to God's word.

If you were to go through the city streets of Scotland today you wouldn't find much that was godly about them – Scotland can't be called The Land of the Book any more. If you can tell where someone comes from by their words, you can also tell a lot about someone by their actions and what they do.

Let's pray that your country and this country of Scotland will one day be brought back to God – so that other countries will look at the things we do and the words we say and they will know how wonderful God is.

Purple Heather

If you visit Scotland and the Highlands during the months of

August and September you should visit the mountains. You will

see a wonderful colourful display – a swathe of purple covering

the hills – because the heather is in bloom.

The heather plant is one that has made Scotland famous and

songs and poems written about this country often refer to its beauty. The plant itself grows naturally in pine woods and on a narrow zone just above the tree line in the mountains.

Typically it grows in peaty soil and there is a lot of that soil throughout Scotland. Peat results from the slow decay and breaking down of vegetable matter in cold and wet climates. God has designed the heather plant in such a way that it can survive in a soil that other plants would not appreciate. The peaty soil does not have a lot of nitrogen and is poor quality for growing in – but heather plants use the fungal parasites in their roots to get nitrogen from the air instead.

Heather also has a complicated life cycle. What is a life cycle? Well a simple life cycle might be:

1. The seed is planted.

2. The seed germinates.

3. A young shoot appears.

4. The plant grows to maturity.

5. The plant dies.

However, heather plants have a life of about forty or fifty years and they have distinct phases of growth throughout this period. The plants grow, develop, mature and decay throughout that time – but many landowners in Scotland need to have young heather plants as food for the animals and birds living on the mountains. So in order to get new fresh growth whole areas of mature heather are carefully set alight so that the old heather burns up and the new heather plants can then take root and grow. However, the older heather plants are useful too because the birds that live on the hillsides need the old bushy heather plants to give them cover and protection from predators.

Life cycles are all part of nature. New plants grow from the soil, animals and children are born. All things eventually die and decay. In certain chapters of the Bible there are long lists of names. It may seem boring to read them but these names are important. They tell us that from the moment mankind sinned death came into the world. Each of these people mentioned in those Bible chapters died and other people replaced them.

Death is part of life, and for the most part every one who has died has stayed dead. Once you die you have to face God's judgement. But there is one who has power over life and death and that is the Lord Jesus Christ.

Those who trust in the Lord Jesus when they come into God's courtroom for the final judgement will have Jesus as their advocate – the one who presents their case. God the Father will see his perfect and righteous Son who has obliterated the sins of his people. There will be no sin to punish. Because of what Jesus did on the cross all the sin of God's people has been forgotten and will never be remembered again. What a wonderful promise!

Those who trust in Jesus to save them from their sins can also be certain that one day in the future their bodies will come back to life too and be reunited with their souls. The one who created life has ultimate control over it.

But death is not something to be scared of if you trust in Jesus. You might be frightened of being sick and sore – but once death has happened if you believe and love the Lord Jesus Christ you will be more alive than you ever were before.

Thorny Thistles

Just as the heather plant is seen as an emblem of Scotland so is the thistle. But the thistle is quite a different plant to the heather. Heather plants were used in olden times to make beds out of – but a bed made out of thorny thistles would not be a pleasant thing to lie on!

There are different types of thistles including The Creeping Thistle, The Spear Thistle and The Marsh Thistle – but all three of these types have purple flower heads and some sort of prickly thorn or leaf.

It is perhaps difficult to work out why the nation of Scotland would choose such a prickly plant or weed, as some gardeners call it, for its emblem.

Perhaps the best reason for this is because the flower is good at defending itself.

The nation of Scotland and the Highlands in particular has had to defend itself on many occasions over the centuries.

The thistle probably reminded the Scottish people in years gone by of how they had to use their spears and swords in much the same way that the thistle used its thorns. The thistle scratches and pierces anyone who wants to dig it up or destroy it. The thistle is a plant with miniature spears all over it. Often Highland families had to fight their enemies in order to be able to stay and live on the land that was theirs. Sometimes they defeated their enemies and sometimes they didn't. Sometimes the Scots had

the strength to fight but sometimes there was nothing they could do. Many crofters were forced off their land during a time called The Clearances. Which is why there are so many people around the world who can trace their roots back to Scotland. Their ancestors left their homes in order to make better lives elsewhere in the world. They had to sail oceans and trek through inhospitable lands in order to find freedom. Many of them longed to go back to the land of their birth but not many did. So throughout the world the emblem of the thistle stands for courage and determination to many people whose forebears left Scotland even though it was the land they called home.

Christians have emblems too to remind them of things. One of these emblems is a cross because Jesus was put to death on a cross.

However, though evil people killed him, his death was actually part of an amazing plan to save sinners – a plan originated by God the Father. Read John 3:16–17 'For God so loved the world that he gave his one and only son that whoever believes in him should not perish but have everlasting life. For God did not send his son into the world to condemn the world but that the world, through him, might be saved.'

The anger of God was poured out on God's Son instead of us so that we can be forgiven of sin and given eternal life. The cross reminds us of God's amazing love. Remember that the cross is an empty cross. The emblem shows us that God did in fact raise Jesus from the dead. Death is not the end of life for a Christian – only the beginning of a better one – the best life of all – eternal life with God.

Now let's get back to the thistle because that little plant can also remind you about things that God wants you to know.

The thistle's thorns can remind you of the crown of thorns that Jesus was forced to wear on his head before he died. Jesus suffered pain for his people. The thorns can also remind us that just as the thistle defends itself against its enemies we need to be defended against sin, temptation and the Devil.

The best way for Christians to defend themselves is to pray to God for help and to read the Bible. God is always listening and ready to deliver you from trouble. God gives you advice and help in his word.

But don't think that when you are struggling with sin that God has forgotten you. He hasn't. God only allows you to be tempted to a certain level. He knows what you can cope with. Don't blame God for your troubles either. Difficulties come into our lives because of humanity's sin. But our God is a great God: he is with us, loving us and strengthening us even in the middle of the greatest struggles and problems.

The Eagle's Eyrie

The Highlands of Scotland have many native birds living in its mountains and glens. Capercaillie are large birds, about the size of a turkey, and they live in the woods of the Eastern Highlands. The huge dark males are unmistakable, but the females look similar to female grouse – another species of bird that lives in the Highlands. Capercaillie are fairly wide spread in Northern and Eastern Europe. If you want to find out how many capercaillie are living in an area the best way is to watch out for the droppings that they leave behind. The droppings are notable as they largely consist of conifer needles.

In contrast to the capercaillie the red grouse is a species of bird that is only found in the British Isles. It has dark wings and a dark rather square tail, but the male has a

little red comb on its head. The capercaillie

on right here and the grouse below both

belong to a class of birds that live in the

wild but are often bred by land owners in

order to be shot later on for food.

However, there is one species of bird that can only be described

as truly wild. It is a bird of prey – the golden eagle. In the past

you might have had more of a chance to see this majestic bird

swooping on its prey as it made its way through the valleys and

glens of Scotland. Now, however, this bird is largely a mountain

bird and there are in fact only 420 pairs left in the United Kingdom,

although they are living and breeding in other European countries.

So it is considerably more difficult to come across one on your

day-to-day travels around the Highlands.

You may, however, get an opportunity so

keep your eyes peeled and keep looking

up. They are usually seen high overhead.

Scan the sky and hilltops. You are more likely to catch sight of one when it is flying. However, don't get confused between the golden eagle and the much smaller, but far more common buzzard.

It can be hard to judge what size a bird is when you are looking into the distance. Just remember that the wing span of the golden eagle is huge (even at a distance), wings look broad and the outer feathers are splayed-out when flying, the tail is wedge-shaped and plumage is medium brown.

Successful breeding pairs are usually found where mountain hares, young deer or grouse are plentiful. Adult golden eagles vary in size. Their length can be anything from 66 to 100 centimetres, the wingspan may be between 150 to 240 centimetres and a weight of 2.5 to 7 kilograms. As in all birds of prey, the females are slightly larger than the males. The plumage ranges from black-brown to dark brown, with a golden-buff crown and nape, which give the bird its name.

If it is an eagle it will be hunting along a hillside, flying low, with deep and powerful wing beats. It will come at its prey – striking it with its feet while still moving at great speed. During the attack eagles are usually silent so as to give them the benefit of surprise. They must get back to their nest or eyrie with a good dinner for their young chicks. Often golden eagles work as a team while hunting: one partner drives the prey to the other partner. They have good eyesight and can spot prey from a long distance. It is believed that they can in fact see detail several times better than humans and are able to spot a rabbit 2 kilometres away. In addition to that eagles are also equipped with a great set of talons. These are thought to be more powerful than the hand and arm strength of any human being. These birds have been perfectly designed to hunt and survive in mountainous conditions. God has seen to it that these birds are well insulated with well over 2000 feathers.

So it goes without saying that the eagle is a splendid bird of prey – but they are sensitive to disturbance which is why you should not approach a nest or eyrie during the months of February and March when the incubating eggs can become quickly chilled. It's hard enough for eagles to survive in such hard climates without the next generation of eagles being killed off because of human interference.

The Bible refers to the strength and magnificence of the eagle. God even described himself as an eagle when he spoke to the Israelites who had been captives of the Egyptians for many years. Finally God arranged it so that his people could escape their slave masters and leave to go to a land of their own. God reminded them in Exodus 19:4 that he had delivered them from the Egyptians. He had rescued them. That is was just as though he had swooped down like an eagle – and instead of destroying them – he had carried them off on his wings to safety.

Safety is definitely something to be thankful for. God has given us safety in many different ways – but the most important way – more important than any other is how he can save us from sin and eternal punishment. But God also tells us that we can be like eagles. Sometimes if we are tired, weary and struggling with life it can be hard to muster any strength to do anything. But that is when God is at his best – he gives strength to the weak and the troubled. If we ask him for help he is always at hand to give us the strength we need and deliver us. We must give him the glory though. If we truly ask God to help us God will give us new strength and we'll be able to get up and do great things for God in his strength. God's strength is glorious and powerful – like an eagle's. If we trust God and turn to him for help we will be as powerful as the eagle, we will keep going and we won't give up.

'But they who wait for the LORD shall renew their strength; they shall mount up with wings like eagles; they shall run and not be weary; they shall walk and not faint' (Isaiah 40:31).

The Highlands and Islands

Two islands off the North-East Coast of Scotland are Orkney and Shetland. If you are planning a visit to Shetland you will have to sail in a ferry overnight from Aberdeen.

There are lots of things to see in Shetland. Its scenery is rugged and beautiful and its wildlife is spectacular, in particular its colonies of bird life such as puffins and skua. But perhaps Shetland is best known for another animal simply because of its name: Shetland pony. This miniature pony can be seen throughout the islands – grazing by the roadside. You might think that it is wild by its appearance. However, the ponies are, in fact, all owned by local crofters.

As a child my parents once took our family on holiday to the Shetlands. I can't remember much about the holiday except for the fact that I was obsessed with Shetland ponies and was determined to take a baby pony back with me in the boot of the car. This never happened needless to say – but I'd given up the idea of a pet pony by the end of the week anyway. I'd come to realise that some ponies are nice and others can have a mean streak to them.

While we visited one of the local women who was known for knitting wonderful woollen jerseys and hats I was told to stay in the garden but not to go anywhere near the pony that was tied to the washing line.

The owner told us, 'He has a mean temper and he'll kick you if you give him a chance.' Ignoring the instructions, as soon as my mother had gone inside the house, I went right up to the pony. I thought I was far enough away to avoid its hooves – but I was wrong. The pony raised its back legs and quickly I turned to run away from it – but I wasn't quick enough. Two hard little hooves went whack into my bottom and I had a big bruise for weeks!

I should have known better. I had been told not to go near the pony. I suppose I thought that since I couldn't touch the pony from where I was standing then it was alright. Unfortunately the pony was near enough not only to touch me – but to give me rather a big bruising.

The lesson I should have learned that day was to obey my parents, but as well as that it teaches me something about sin. Often we can want to do something that is against God's law – so we think about it and about how it might be fun to do what we want. When we think about this particular sin then we start to think about it some more, we maybe become friends with people who think the same way. Perhaps these people are heavily involved in that particular sin and they think that we should just join in. The Bible tells us that we are to flee from the evil desires of youth, from immorality, from the love of money. The word flee means to run for your life – sin is dangerous. If you sit around thinking about sin, if you feel yourself tempted to sin and do nothing to get away then sin will catch you and before you know it you'll be doing that sin and not just thinking about it. The Shetland pony gave me a sore reminder that unless I obey I can get hurt.

Because Shetland is situated in the middle of the North Sea it is just as close to Norway as it is to Scotland and this is reflected in its culture. There is a lot of Viking history in Shetland. Every year the residents of the island celebrate their Viking roots by building a replica Viking warship and burning it with torches. This festival is called *Up Helly Aa* and is held annually in the middle of winter. After nightfall the Viking ship is dragged through the streets of the town in a torchlight procession, with everyone dressed in costumes. After the singing of the *Up Helly Aa* song, the torches are thrown into the warship to set it ablaze.

But there is another part of Shetland's history that is more worthy of note than even the Vikings. Last century during the 1940s Europe was involved in a bitter conflict which is now called The Second World War. In 1940 German forces occupied the land of Norway resulting in a stream of refugees from that country. Many ended up in Shetland. It wasn't long before Norway surrendered completely to the occupying forces and those Norwegians who had escaped to Shetland began to plan a resistance movement. The Norwegians began to train alongside the British armed forces. They knew that in their country there were thousands of Norwegian servicemen in hiding. These soldiers only needed arms and communications and they would become an effective opposition to the occupying army.

During 1941 and under the leadership of men like Lief Lars many successful missions were carried out. The crossings were often made during the winter. Because of the lack of sunshine hours during the Northern winters this meant that the Norwegian coast was reached under the cover of darkness. Crews and passengers had to endure North Sea storms with no lights, and a constant risk of discovery by German planes or boats. It was decided that the boats should be disguised as working fishing boats and the crew as fishermen, in waterproofs. These small fishing-boats were the crucial link in the chain between Norway and the allied forces. They were the only way for agents, radio sets and ammunition to reach the underground Norwegian army.

The whole operation came to be known as The Shetland Bus and it is an example of how ordinary people can do heroic and selfless deeds in order to help others.

It wasn't really until the Second World War ended that people began to realise the significance of The Shetland Bus and the secret missions that had been originated on the island. Because of the great level of activity and opposition shown by these missions the German High Command were convinced that the allied invasion would come through Norway instead of through France. When the Allies invaded Normandy in June 1944 as many as 340,000 German troops and a large part of the German Navy were stationed in Norway with little chance of getting out.

When the Germans surrendered in May 1945 it was discovered that Norway had sixty illegal radio stations and most of them had got their equipment from Shetland.

We talked about how we have to flee from sin and immorality. The Norwegian people and the Shetlanders understood what it meant to flee from danger. They had to flee for their lives from the occupying forces, they had to rescue people and take them to safety, they had to fight their enemies. The Bible tells us that we are to flee from the wrath to come. Wrath is another word for anger and the anger we are to flee is God's anger. The farthest northerly point on mainland Scotland is Cape Wrath. When storms crash against the cliffs you can see how that place got its name. The scenery looks angry and fierce. God is angry at sin and one day sin will be punished. If you die without believing in Christ your sin will be punished. However, until that day you are being given an opportunity to flee from God's anger to God's love. God offers you love and forgiveness through his Son, Jesus Christ. When the

Lord Jesus died on the cross he made it possible for you to flee to safety. Those who believe in Jesus and trust him to save them will be safe in heaven when they die. In the Bible God's anger is described as the anger to come – that means it is in the future still. If you are alive but have not trusted in Christ, God's anger is in the future – and if you die without Christ, God's anger will be in the future forever. But you still have a chance to flee to God to ask for forgiveness and if you do that God's anger will not be an anger raised against you because you will be his child, a member of his family – one that he will save and protect and defend whatever happens.

The Road to The West

The West Coast of Scotland is a favourite tourist attraction. Many people go there to see the spectacular mountains and deep sea lochs. They may also hope to catch sight of one of Scotland's most magnificent animals, the red deer stag.

The average male is about 1.2 metres high and weighs 295 kilograms. Look out for them particularly in the winter months as the herds of wild deer will make their way down from the heights to the lower valleys in order to find food. Be particularly aware, however, if you are driving through the Highlands at night as many road accidents occur as a result of cars colliding with deer. In fact a friend of my family was driving home one night when his Volvo ran straight into a large stag. The animal's body went right over the car roof, its antlers then breaking through the rear window. Thankfully our friend had been travelling alone, if he had had any passengers with him they would certainly have been killed.

Mature red deer usually stay in single-sex groups for most of the year. During the mating ritual, called the rut, mature stags compete for the attentions of the female hinds and will try to defend the hinds that they attract. Rival stags will challenge their opponents by bellowing and walking in full view of the other stag. This allows the two males to assess each other's body size and fighting strength. If neither stag backs down a clash of antlers occurs. Sometimes during these combats stags can sustain serious injuries.

Red stags are truly majestic when they are carrying a full 'rack' of antlers. It is a sight that inspired the artist Landseer to paint one of the most famous animal portraits of all time, *Monarch of the Glen.*

Red deer that live in the Lowlands can grow far more points on their antlers than those in the Highlands. The better Highland stags

will grow twelve points to their antlers and when this is achieved they also attain the name of 'Royal'. The wonderful Monarch of the Glen, however, needs a lot of nutrition to be able to grow this remarkable set of antlers. He is only really the unchallenged monarch of the glen because he has no natural predators. Ever since wolves died out in Scotland the red deer population has pretty much remained unchecked. That is why land owners have to organise red deer culls each year. Have you ever eaten the meat that comes from red deer? Venison is increasing in popularity due to its low fat content – so if you get a chance try some when you are in the Highlands.

From the West Coast it is an easy journey to the island of Skye which is famous for its mountains and its music. A three hour ferry journey will then take you to the islands of Lewis, Harris and Uist. However, if you want to get to St. Kilda, which is further west, then you might have to take a helicopter.

On the Island of Skye the Cuillins attract the most attention, particularly those mountains known as the Black Cuillin. The summits are bare rock, jagged in outline and with many steep cliffs and deep corries.

Throughout Scotland mountaineers and hikers refer to mountains of over 3000 feet as Munros. People who aim to climb as many of these mountains as possible are nick-named Munro-baggers. There are 284 Munros and they are the highest of Scotland's mountains. They are named after the man who first catalogued them, Sir Hugh Munro. All twelve Munros on Skye are Black Cuillin peaks and are amongst the most challenging hills in the British Isles. Several of the summits require rock-climbing skills in order to ascend in safety.

The Cuillin Ridge itself is only seven miles in length but on average it takes fifteen to twenty hours to cross this difficult terrain. However, the current record to cross from one side to the other stands at around three and a half hours. Mountain climbers who tackle this ridge face a further complication, which is the lack of any source of water on the ridge itself. This means that if you are going to cross the ridge all your water must be carried with you in order to avoid having to descend for water and climb back up later.

The Cuillins are perhaps the only range in the U.K. that rival the Alps as a mountaineering challenge, but these mountains do not have the same severe winter weather conditions.

Many people know of the Island of Skye through the popular folk-song *The Skye Boat Song*, a song that arose around the legend of Bonnie Prince Charlie. This particular prince had raised an army to fight against the government forces in order that his family could seize the crown. Many Highlanders supported his cause as they believed that he was the true heir to the throne. These men were called Jacobites and the Jacobite army fought its way through Scotland and England and only had to turn back when it ran out of steam just short of London. The final story of the Jacobite rebellion took place at the Battle of Culloden in 1745, just a few miles out of the City of Inverness. Here the Jacobite forces were defeated and the Highland warriors subdued. Many had to face the fury of the government troops but Bonnie Prince Charlie escaped by sailing on a boat to Skye disguised as a female servant of a woman named Flora MacDonald. Later he travelled to Rome and died an alcoholic. Many of his followers were killed, imprisoned or emigrated to America to set up new lives for themselves.

One of the verses of *The Skye Boat Song* has the words, 'Where is the lad that is born to be king?'

For Christians there is only one who is truly born to be king over our lives, and that one is Jesus Christ. He was born in a stable in Bethlehem, which is unusual for a king. He lived a life of poverty, was put to death on a cross, and was raised from the dead three days later. Is he king of your life? Have you asked God to forgive you in the name of Jesus? If he isn't king of your life then you are in opposition to him and you are on the side of the enemy instead of the side of heaven. It is important to realise that in this battle the enemy's side is the losing side.

Jesus Christ has many different titles one of which is King of kings and Lord of lords. There is no ruler who is more powerful than him and one day that will be proven when he returns. The baby who was born in a manger, the Saviour who died on the cross, will return to judge the world, he will return as a victorious and glorious King!

The Monarch of the Glen with its rack of antlers may be a magnificent sight but Jesus Christ is the Lord of Glory and the ruler of the universe. He longs to have his people with him in heaven. He longs to talk to you and to bring you to himself. You can come to Jesus at any time, any where – you don't have to wait to go into his throne room as you would have to wait to go into the throne room of a king or queen in this world. Communication with your Lord and Saviour is instant and personal.

One of the islands of the North West of Scotland is the island

of St. Kilda. It is a remote place. No native inhabitants live there any more. Only military personnel and National Trust employees can be found on the island along with some visiting tourists. However, for centuries there was a community of people who lived and worked there, cut off from the rest of the world and often from the rest of Scotland. Their visits to the mainland being infrequent the St. Kildans would often return to their homes with amazing stories of things they had seen and heard of that did not exist on their island – animals such as rabbits and pigs and even bees. Trees didn't grow on St. Kilda either. Very few people could read and write. However, the St. Kildans did have their own songs and stories, their own traditions and even their own parliament. The St. Kilda parliament met every weekday morning where the

men of the community would sit down and decide what work needed to be done that day. There were sheep and other animals to tend to, as well as fish to catch and nets to mend. There were many tasks that this small population had to perform because being so far away from the mainland they had to survive on their own.

This isolation meant that in the case of an emergency the only way to communicate with the mainland was to light a bonfire on top of Conachair in the hope that a passing ship might see the smoke – or to send a letter by St. Kilda mail-boat. Unfortunately this was not a boat with an engine or sail – but simply a letter inserted into a small container and tied to a floating buoy with a little red flag on the top. The buoy was generally made out of a sheep's stomach – something that was readily to hand on the island.

The St. Kildans' first attempt at this form of postage was picked up on the coast of Orkney nine days after they had sent it off. On other occasions the letters would even arrive on the coast of Norway.

It wasn't an easy way to communicate with the outside world, the St. Kildans couldn't even be sure that their letters would even be found, far less arrive at their destination.

So don't you think that it is a great thing to be able to ask someone for help when they are close at hand? Help is always close at hand with God. We don't need to write a letter to him or even dial a telephone to get in touch with him – we simply talk to God and listen to him through his word, the Bible. In fact when we pray to God he knows what we are going to pray to him about before we say a word. He often sends an answer to our prayer before we ask it. When God answers our prayers we realise that

he must have been sending us this help even before we realised that we needed it.

'Before they call I will answer; while they are still speaking I will hear' (Isaiah 65:24).

Highland Warriors

When touring the Highlands you can't get away from history and battles. After the defeat at the Battle of Culloden many Highlanders faced persecution. The Gaelic language was made illegal as was tartan. Bagpipes were no longer allowed because they were the traditional way for the clans to call men to battle.

But there are successful battles that Highlanders fought in – some of which took place in the Lowlands of Scotland long before the Battle of Culloden. The clans from the North would often fight in battles outside their own area when the clan chiefs were called on to fight a common enemy.

The nation of Scotland went through many power struggles in its history. When King Alexander III died without an heir many people laid claim to the throne. King Edward of England was approached by the Scottish nobles and asked to choose the next king. Now Edward wanted to make sure that whoever was chosen as king would be loyal to him and follow his command so he opted for John Balliol. Shortly afterwards however Balliol rebelled against the overrule of King Edward and a battle ensued. King Edward thoroughly defeated the Scottish lords and immediately sent his own nobles to the country to rule the people.

It was during this time that two well-known Scottish heroes arose – William Wallace and Robert the Bruce.

William Wallace was the son of a Renfrewshire knight and refused to stand by while his country was overtaken by a foreign power. Soon he was at the head of an army and the castles that had been taken by the English soldiers came under Scottish control once more. At the Battle of Stirling Bridge in 1297 Wallace fought against the Earl of Surrey who had been left behind by Edward to rule Scotland. The Earl did not want to fight Wallace so when Wallace arrived at Stirling to fight for the castle the Earl immediately sent out two messengers to ask for peace. Wallace replied 'We have not come here to ask for peace but to fight for the freedom of our kingdom.'

The battle went ahead. The English army had to advance two by two across a narrow bridge. Wallace's men seized the bridge and stopped the army from getting across. Only one English horseman made it back across the bridge alive. The battle was a resounding success for Wallace and his men.

However, even though he had sent the English rulers packing Wallace did not declare himself as king: instead he referred to himself as 'The Guardian of the Land.' However, this guardian

was soon on the run for his life. The Scottish battle tactics did not succeed at Falkirk. Most of Wallace's army were armed with spears, few if any fought on horseback. The Scots fought the enemy by standing in a circle formation. Each circle was made up of three ranks. The first rank knelt on the ground holding their spears; the second rank behind them stood up with the spears pointing over the shoulders of the men in front. A third rank stood behind the second rank waiting to take the place of any who were killed or wounded. At first this formation was impenetrable but when Edward ordered his archers to fire arrows into the circles of Scottish fighters, thousands were killed.

Eventually Wallace himself was captured and brought to London to be tried as a traitor. He was of course found guilty and put to death.

The story of The Guardian of the Land had come to an end. Many of his followers would have felt that there was no point in carrying on. What a disappointment for their hopes and dreams of freedom.

When Jesus Christ died on the cross his followers must have felt crushed. Many had thought he would defeat their enemies. Some had wanted to crown him king – but God had a different plan. His plan was to bring salvation to lost sinners. Jesus wasn't going to start an earthly kingdom – but a heavenly one. Jesus' story is so unlike the story of William Wallace. Wallace was

killed and defeated – Jesus was killed and was victorious. How did that happen? On the third day Jesus rose from the dead. The resurrection was witnessed by many – individuals met with him as they travelled, the disciples ate a picnic with him on the beach, crowds of people saw him alive for themselves.

'Jesus said to him, "Have you believed because you have seen me? Blessed are those who have not seen and yet have believed"' (John 20:29).

Highland Refuge

Throughout history many people have found refuge in the Highlands. In the past this was because it was remote, mountainous and easy to hide in. After William Wallace was killed another Scottish hero replaced him. This time it was a hero with a claim to the throne – Robert the Bruce. It wasn't long before he had to flee for his life to the Highlands and then to the Western Isles. He had been crowned King of Scotland so now King Edward wanted him dead.

Robert escaped the clutches of one soldier by untying his cloak and running for the hills. The soldier was left behind with just Robert's cloak flapping in the breeze. Another time a blood

hound was used by Robert's enemies to track him down. But Robert waded through a stream to put the hound off the scent and evaded his enemies by stealth and skill. He fought them off with his broadsword and tricked them with his cunning.

There is a story told about when Robert was hiding from his enemies in a cave. He was cold and depressed and afraid. There seemed to be nothing that he could do to get away from his enemies. Would he ever be able to rule Scotland? Would his country ever be free? Robert felt like giving up: but a shaft of light brought his attention to a little spider that had just fallen off the top of one of the rocks in the cave. It was trying to make a web and would not give up even though it fell again and again. Undeterred, for the third time the spider began its way to the top and eventually managed to build its web. Robert sat in wonder! This was what he needed to do – he would not give up on Scotland. He would keep going and would persevere.

Do you ever feel like giving up? You may not have an army chasing you – but sometimes life can be full of other sorts of challenges. The Bible tells us that we shouldn't give up: 'Let us not grow weary of doing good, for in due season we will reap, if we do not give up' (Galatians 6:9). If you keep doing the good works that God has given you to do then in the future you will be rewarded. God has promised a reward to his people. They have been given the free gift of eternal life already but there will be many more blessings for God's faithful people in heaven.

Robert the Bruce eventually defeated King Edward's army at the battle of Bannockburn. On the day of the battle when the two armies faced each other King Edward saw the Scottish forces getting down on their knees – at first he thought they might be pleading for mercy – but then he realised they were kneeling in prayer to God. Immediately Edward gave the order to attack. But no matter how many times they charged the

Scottish spears withstood them. The boggy conditions and the lie of the land made it difficult for the English army to bring in reinforcements. When the English forces were pushed back into the marshes Robert the Bruce gave a great shout. From behind the Scottish warriors a large crowd emerged shouting and waving flags and banners. The discouraged English forces were sure that the Scots had called for reinforcements. The cheering crowd charged and the English army scattered.

What the English hadn't realised was that the new arrivals were in fact unarmed camp followers, women and children who followed the Scottish troops around the country. Soon the Scottish forces had soundly defeated their enemies and Edward was fleeing for his life.

Perhaps the Scottish soldiers recognised the fact that God had helped them win the battle? Perhaps they felt in the end that it was their own clever tactics that won the day. But in the book of Proverbs we are told to acknowledge God. 'In all your ways acknowledge him and he will direct your paths.' Too often we can run to God with our problems and when things go well we think that we don't need him.

It is the Lord God who gives you every good and perfect gift. God has given us the best and the most perfect gift in Jesus Christ his Son.

'For God so loved the world that he gave his only Son, that whoever believes in him should not perish but have eternal life. For God did not send his Son into the world to condemn the world, but in order that the world might be saved through him' (John 3:16-17).

Sea Life

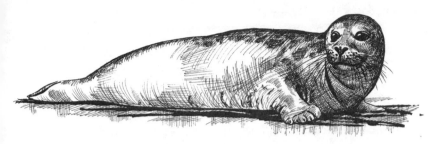

In the Highlands of Scotland the nature and wildlife of the area is varied in ways that you will not experience in other countries. This is simply because Scotland is both a high mountainous country as well as part of an island. So as well as having high ground it also has a craggy coast land, with miles of beaches and sea lochs.

The marine life around the shores of Scotland is magnificent. On the East Coast in the Moray Firth you will find one of the U.K.'s few resident communities of dolphin, numbering close to 130 members. Bottlenose dolphins, though they may resemble fish, are small whales and are warm-blooded mammals. They breathe air like mammals and bear live young, suckling them for up to four years after birth.

Dolphins are whales with teeth and actively pursue and catch their prey, consisting of salmon, herring, mackerel and other fish. Long before human beings had invented sonar to help submarines detect objects under water God had designed a sonar system for the dolphin in order to help it hunt. The dolphin issues a series of clicks and the sound echoes off the objects round about it so that it can hunt its prey with ease.

Dolphins have few animal predators and the biggest threat to their existence is from man. They can get tangled up in nets and often suffer from pollution or disturbance from boats. So this is why if you want to see the dolphins the best place is either from a recognised lookout point or on an officially registered dolphin cruise.

Other ocean life is plentiful such as seals. You will see many basking in the sunlight on the rocks along the coast, enjoying a sunbathe in much the same way as tourists enjoy basking in the sun on their holidays.

Another aquatic life form is both wild and farmed in Scotland – this is salmon. It is caught at sea in nets and in fresh water by line

fishing. Wild salmon come from the sea to the rivers every year in order to breed or spawn. The fish make the return journey to the river beds every year and it is a long and tiring journey for them as they journey against the current. Leaping and diving up waterfalls they make a spectacular sight. They are driven by a natural urge to return to the spawning ground that they left many years before as young smolts. During the five or so years that they swim around the Atlantic covering thousands of miles the smolts mature into adult salmon and then return to mate for themselves. However, for many of these salmon this will only happen once because weeks after they mate most will die, never to return to the sea.

It is amazing to think of these fish and their determination to return to the river beds from which they came. We might describe it as a longing. Human beings often long to return to their homes after a long time away. That can be a joyful occasion. Something that is even more joyful though is returning to God. If you have never known the joy of being in God's family then you should really turn to God now and ask him to forgive you for your sin.

The joy of forgiveness and belonging to God is a joy that will last forever – not just for a day or two.

Sometimes Christians can wander away from God. Perhaps you once loved God but now you find that you don't want to follow his ways or to enjoy his company. In the Bible Jesus describes people like this as having left their first love. Jesus should be the most important one in our lives – the one we long to be with most of all. The salmon long to return to the river beds – Christians should long even more to be with God and to worship him.

Lochs and Legends

As well as spectacular mountains and coastlines the Highlands of Scotland have a large selection of fresh water lakes or lochs. Loch is the Scottish word for lake and is pronounced with a rolling, throaty sound at the end of the word.

Many of the lochs in Scotland have mysterious legends told about them. One legend brings people back to the Highlands again and again. It is perhaps the Highlands most popular tourist attraction as many people want to spot the Loch Ness Monster, also known as Nessie.

Loch Ness is the second largest loch by surface area in the U.K. but due to its extreme depth it is the loch with the largest volume of water. Due to the peat in the surrounding area the water is a dark murky colour so it is difficult to see into its depths with the naked eye. However, several major sonar scans have taken place in order to hunt the elusive beast down but nothing has been proven either way. In 1987 Operation Deepscan covered the entire surface of the loch with twenty motor cruisers, creating a sonar envelope from which 'nothing' could hide. Nessie, however, did. And it is agreed that underwater caves, impenetrable to sonar beams could give Nessie some ideal hiding places.

There are people who don't believe in Nessie but they like the fact that the monster is good for tourism! Whether you believe there is a monster or not doesn't really matter – what does matter is if you believe in God. The Bible has one thing to say to people who do not believe in the Lord God: 'The fool says in his heart that there is no God' Psalm 14:1. And it is remarkably foolish to say that God doesn't exist when you look at his creation. Here you witness wonderful scenery, amazing animals and wildlife. Creation is evidence for the existence of the Creator. Designs

do not happen by chance – they have to be designed. Throw the parts of a watch into a shoe box and shake it randomly. It doesn't matter how many times you open the shoe box the watch parts will never suddenly come together of their own accord or by chance into a perfectly working mechanism. Yet people assume that fully functioning animals, plants and the whole of creation came together as a result of chance, a big bang mixed in with a liberal doze of millions of years! No – it just isn't going to happen no matter how many millions of years you add on!

But here is the real reason you should believe in God. You should believe in God because of God himself, the truth he has given us and the witness of his people. He is here, with us.

How else could a ramshackle group of fishermen from a little country on the outskirts of Africa change from being nervous cowards to bold evangelists spreading the good news of the resurrection of Jesus Christ?

The living, loving, Lord Jesus Christ, the son of God, did die and did rise from the dead!

People's lives are changed all over the world because of the power of the word of God.

In Scotland you will see lots of plants and trees — but there is a tree that is quite rare — a Scots pine. Look out for it when you visit — it is tall and straight with most of its foliage near the top. Next time you walk through a forest or wooded area look at the effect the wind has on the branches. You can't see the wind but you can see the wind at work as it blows in the trees, lifting leaves up off the ground and bending branches.

Another way you can see the wind at work is when you see it turning round the arms of a windmill. Windmills are becoming more common in the Highlands of Scotland and actually cause some heated arguments. Some people hate the way they look on the hillsides. Some people are more concerned about having another source for energy other than gas and oil. But you can see these modern wind turbines high up on the mountain tops and they are being used to generate electricity.

Whenever you see the wind at work remember that you can't see God either but you can see God at work in the lives of people. Before when they didn't know God they had no hope or joy – now

that they have had their sins forgiven and know for sure that God exists because they have met with him – they have hope and they have joy – in truckloads!

When I was young my family would often drive down the A9 from Inverness to Glasgow to go and visit my grandmother. One of the games my sisters and I would do to amuse ourselves on the long journey would be to count how many waterfalls we could see. We would always arrive at quite a high number. There is plenty of fresh mountain water to be had in the Highlands. In fact when my sisters and I were visiting my other granny near the Cromarty Firth we went on a walk to a special place called 'The Well of Health'. It was quite a long walk and by the end we were very thirsty and glad to get a fresh cool drink of water from the well. It was called 'The Well of Health' because the water was supposed to make you strong. However, in the book of Revelation in the Bible we are told that there is water of life flowing from the throne of God, a true and living water. 'Then the angel showed me the river of the water of life, bright as crystal, flowing from the throne of God and of the Lamb' Revelation 22:1.

And in John 7:38 we read that Jesus said: 'Whoever believes in me, as the Scripture has said, "Out of his heart will flow rivers of living water."'

When you taste the cool fresh waters of the Highlands for the first time remember this – that once you have drunk this water you will be thirsty again in a few hours time. But for your thirsty soul there is only one water to drink and that is the water that Jesus Christ gives – one drink of that and your soul will never be thirsty again.

Tourist Information

For those of you who are planning a visit to the Highlands of Scotland the following web pages offer helpful information

www.visithighlands.com

www.visitscotland.com

These web sites offer information on accommodation, travel arrangements, car-hire and visitor attractions, as well as giving internet links to other appropriate web sites.

Prior to visiting any internet site please ensure that your family is web-aware. Children should be supervised on line or you should have appropriate internet security installed.

Wherever you travel in the Highlands, you're never far from local information and friendly advice. All official tourist outlets offer leaflets, brochures and assistance. Tourist information offices will help you to make the most of your time in the Highlands. Look for the "i" signpost at any of the following locations:

Achnasheen, Applecross
Beauly, Bettyhill, Broadford, Brora, Cluanie
Daviot Wood, Dornoch, Dunbeath, Dunnet
Dunvegan, Durness, Drumnadrochit
Fort Augustus, Gairloch, Golspie
Inverness, Isle of Raasay
John o' Groats, Kinlochbervie, Kyle of Lochalsh
Lairg, Latheron, Lochinver
Nairn, North Kessock
Plockton, Portree
Strathcarron, Strathpeffer
Tain, Thurso, Tongue
Uig, Ullapool, Wick

To find routes and distances between places within the U.K. visit www.theaa.com

For information on public transport visit www.travelinescotland.com

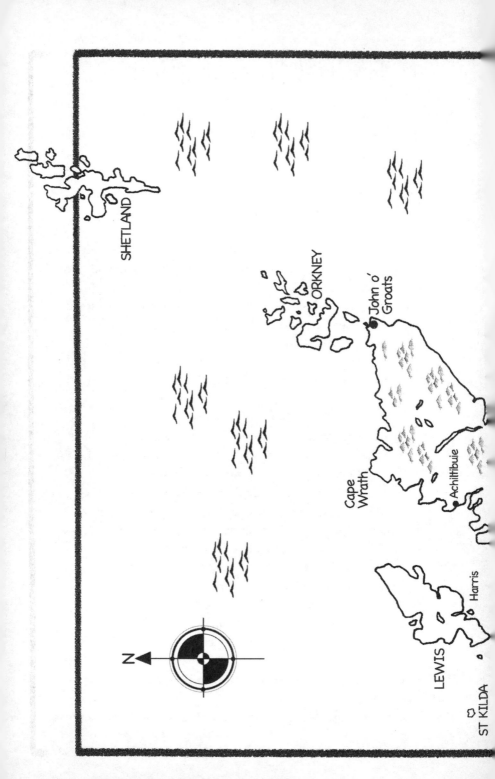

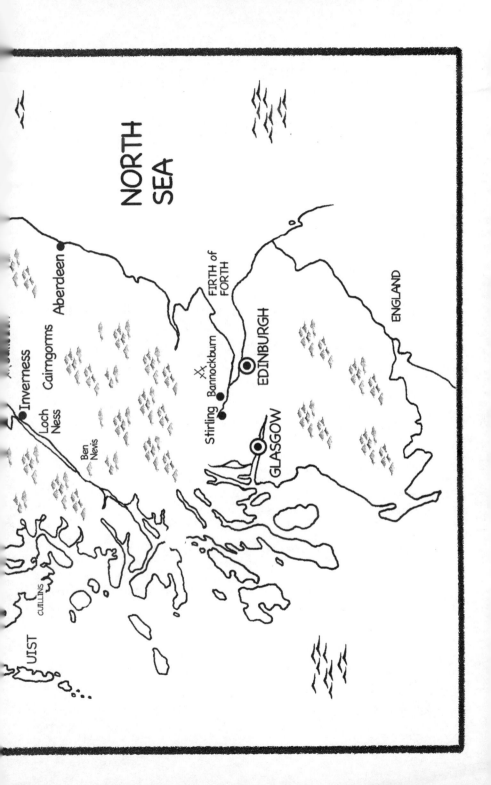

Scottish Highland Adventures Quiz

1. How many welcomes might you get in the Highlands?

2. Who does God forgive willingly?

3. What is the highest mountain in the U.K.?

4. What poisons our hearts so we don't want to please God?

5. What language was spoken in Scotland 200 years ago?

6. What was Scotland once known as?

7. What kind of soil does heather grow in?

8. What do we all have to face after death?

9. What happened during The Clearances?

10. What does the empty cross remind us of?

11. What should you look for in order to work out how many capercaillie are in your area?

12. God is strong and powerful. What powerful bird does God compare himself to?

13. What island has a pony and a bus named after it?

14. What is another word that you can use instead of the word wrath?

15. What name is given to a red deer stag with twelve points to its antlers?

16. Why was it strange that Jesus was born in a stable?

17. Who was known as 'The Guardian of the Land'?

18. How was Jesus victorious even though he died?

19. What animal inspired Robert the Bruce?

20. Who gives us every good and perfect gift?

21. Are dolphins fish or mammals?

22. Salmon long to return to the river beds. Who should Christians long to return to?

23. What makes Loch Ness a dark murky colour?

24. Who says in his heart there is no God?

Scottish Highland Adventures Answers

1. One hundred thousand.

2. All those who trust in him.

3. Ben Nevis.

4. Sin.

5. Gaelic.

6. The Land of the Book.

7. Peaty soil.

8. God's judgement.

9. Crofters were forced off their land.

10. Jesus has risen from the dead.

11. Their droppings.

12. The eagle.

13. Shetland.

14. Anger.

15. Royal.

16. He was the King of kings.

17. William Wallace.

18. He defeated sin and rose from the dead.

19. A spider.

20. God.

21. Mammals.

22. The Lord Jesus.

23. Peat.

24. The fool.

Himalayan Adventures
by Penny Reeve

Do you like mountain climbing or trekking? If so, then you will love to explore in the Himalayan countries such as India and Nepal where you will find elephants and tigers galore. As you meet fascinating people, you will see God at work in these people and creation too.

ISBN: 978-1-84550-080-1

Wild West Adventures
by Donna Vann

Wild West country sretches from Mississippi River to the

Pacific Ocean. Incredible stories from the Wild West about the

animals and scenery and of people of faith who were inspired

by Jesus.

ISBN: 978-1-84550-065-8

Author Information: Catherine Mackenzie

Catherine Mackenzie lives and works in the Highlands of Scotland. She has written several books for children from pre-school to teenagers. She is involved in children's work at her local church and enjoys reading stories to and playing games with her growing number of nephews and nieces.

Catherine has loved books for as long as she can remember. Aged four the only way her parents could get her to swallow some hideously pink medicine was to promise her a book if she took it. She gave in, swallowed and got her book.

Books have played an important part in her life ever since. They have inspired her, helped increase her over-active imagination, and taught her about the Lord Jesus Christ and her need of him.

Other books by Catherine Mackenzie

TALES FROM CANTERBURY PLACE

The Big Green Tree at Number 11 - ISBN: 978-185792-7313

The Dark Blue Bike at Number 17 - ISBN: 978-185792-7320

The Deep Black Pond at Number 12 - ISBN: 978-185792-7337

The Lonely Grey Dog at Number 6 - ISBN: 978-184550-1037

TRAILBLAZERS

Swimming against the Tide: Joni Eareckson Tada

ISBN: 978-185792-8334

Servant to the Slave: Mary Slessor

ISBN: 978-185792-3483

An Adventure Begins: Hudson Taylor

ISBN: 978-185792-4237

A Voice in the Dark: Richard Wurmbrand

ISBN: 978-185792-2981

CF 4•K

Because you're never
too young to know Jesus

Christian Focus Publications publishes books for adults and children under its three main imprints: Christian Focus, Mentor and Christian Heritage. Our books reflect that God's word is reliable and Jesus is the way to know him, and live for ever with him. Our children's publication list includes a Sunday school curriculum that covers pre-school to early teens; puzzle and activity books. We also publish personal and family devotional titles, biographies and inspirational stories that children will love. If you are looking for quality Bible teaching for children then we have an excellent range of Bible story and age specific theological books. From pre-school to teenage fiction, we have it covered!

Find us at our webpage:
www.christianfocus.com

CHRISTIAN FOCUS PUBLICATIONS

Christian Christian   CF4K Mentor
Focus   Heritage